The Color of Us

The Color of Us

by Kathy Hardee

with pictures by Susie Rogers

kathy@kathyhardee.com

Illustrator: Susie Rogers

Published by Redemption Press, PO Box 427, Enumclaw, WA 98022

Toll Free (844) 2REDEEM (273-3336)

Redemption Press is honored to present this title in partnership with the author. The views expressed or implied in this work are those of the author. Redemption Press provides our imprint seal representing design excellence, creative content and high quality production.

All Scripture quotations are taken from The Holy Bible: English Standard Version, copyright © 2001, Wheaton: Good News Publishers. Used by permission. All rights reserved.

ISBN: 978-1-68314-842-5

Library of Congress Catalog Card Number: 2018963931

We dedicate this little book to our great big God, who made us exactly the way He wanted us to be.

I praise you, for I am fearfully and wonderfully made. Wonderful are your works; my soul knows it very well. Psalm 139:14

Come along with
me and see
why we are
colored differently.

Think with me, see if you can,
back to when God first made man.

Not too dark and
not too light,
God made Adam's
skin just right.

That's how all God's people were,
but none were ever born with fur.

God mixed up some melanin
to make the color of our skin.

My friend
Matthew has a lot,
but Isabella
sure does not.

When God started making you,
He knew exactly what to do.

Draw or paste a picture of yourself in the frame.

Olive skin and coal-black hair,
God's designs are everywhere.

Skin that's blue or gray or green?
Those are shades I've never seen!

Curly locks and dark brown eyes—
every child is God's surprise.

Some are dark and some quite fair.
God creates each one with care.

Some are blond and some brunett.
God decides the shades we get.

Rosy hair and freckles too—
aren't you glad that God made you?

Spiky hair that stands up straight—
God made you! Let's celebrate!

Hoot and holler. Jump for joy.

God loves every girl and boy!

Choruses for You to Sing

Jesus Made Me
Sing to the tune of "Jesus Loves Me."

Jesus made me, this I know,
for the Bible tells me so;
He created everything,
that is why to Him we sing.
Yes, Jesus made me.
Yes, Jesus made me.
Yes, Jesus made me.
The Bible tells me so.

God M-A-D-E Me
Sing to the tune of "The B-I-B-L-E."

God m-a-d-e me.
I'm special can't you see?
I will believe in the Lord my God;
He m-a-d-e me!

Jesus Made the Little Children
Sing to the tune of "Jesus Loves the Little Children."

Jesus made the little children,
all the children of the world.
He created you and me with originality.
Jesus made the little children of the world.

Hi! I'm Kathy.
Susie and I had so much fun
working on this book for you.
We hope you like the story,
songs, and pictures!

Susie

NOTE TO PARENTS

In the Bible there are no races, just people living in different places.

God gave Adam a flawless gene pool. His skin was probably a mid-brown color, perfectly suited for his environment. All human beings are born with the same skin-coloring pigment God gave Adam: melanin. Some people are able to produce more melanin than others.

Nine generations after Adam, Lamech and his wife gave birth to Noah (Genesis 5:28). During Noah's lifetime, God sent a worldwide flood. Noah and his family were the only human survivors of the flood. God told them to multiply and fill the earth (Genesis 9:1).

For a few hundred years couples married and had children, and their children had children. They were pleased to multiply, but perfectly content to stay put. They ignored God's command to fill the earth and instead built a great city in rebellion against God.

To get them moving, God confused things by imposing on them different languages. Up until that time, everyone had pretty much the same skin color and spoke the same language.

All of a sudden, one person couldn't understand the other, so they went their separate ways and began to fill the earth. People able to produce a lot of melanin thrived in warm, sunny regions. Those who produced less melanin had a better survival rate in cold regions. After several generations, people who lived in cold climate zones had predominately light skin; people who lived in warm climate zones had predominately dark skin, even though they all originated from the same population (Genesis 11:1-9).

"And he made from one man every nation of mankind to live on all the face of the earth" (Acts 17:26).

For more information visit answersingenesis.org.

ORDER INFORMATION

To order additional copies of this book, please visit
www.redemption-press.com.

Also available on Amazon.com and BarnesandNoble.com
or by calling toll-free 1-844-2REDEEM.

CPSIA information can be obtained
at www.ICGtesting.com
Printed in the USA
BVHW061150020419
544328BV00001BA/5/P